Aubi

David Batten

Cinnamon Press
:: small miracles from distinctive voices ::

Published by Cinnamon Press
www.cinnamonpress.com

The right of David Batten to be identified as author of this work has been asserted by him in accordance with the Copyright, Designs and Patent Act, 1988. © 2024, David Batten
ISBN 978-1-78864-164-7

British Library Cataloguing in Publication Data. A CIP record for this book can be obtained from the British Library.

Designed and typeset in Bodoni by Cinnamon Press. Cover design by Adam Craig © Adam Craig. Image: Marc Chesneau/iStock

Cinnamon Press is represented by Inpress.

Acknowledgements

Thanks to the editors of *The Dawntreader, Envoi* and *The French Literary Review* and in which some of these poems have appeared.

Previous Publications

Transhumance (Cinnamon Press 2016)
Storme Passage (pamphlet, Cinnamon Press 2017)
Untergang (Cinnamon Press 2018)
Rotterdam (novella, Liquorice Fish Books 2019)
Winterreis (Cinnamon Press 2021)

About the Author

David Batten was educated at Loughborough and Hull and worked in rural development in Gwynedd, North Wales. He now lives with his partner, Ingrid, in the Aveyron, southern France, where he writes, brews beer and works as a *paysagiste*.

Contents

For Nico

1971-2023

fellow Celt

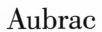

Aubrac

Preface

We aren't a part of nature—we are nature, my starting point for this collection of poems. Aubrac is a geographical area in France bounded by three river gorges at the southern edge of The Massif Central. It comprises the largest volcanic plateau in Europe, rising to over 1400 metres. Very cold in winter, hot in summer, riven by dramatic ravines its pasturelands are ideal summer grazing for the troops of cattle walked up at the end of May where they graze until the end of October and the descent to the winter barns of the deep dark valleys, a transhumance that has been enacted here for at least 3000 years. The herds were no doubt following this pattern before we started following them, from the end of the last ice age.

This was Celtic country, land of the Gauls, who spoke a language similar to that used today in much of rural Wales, before being ransacked by invaders: Romans, Christians, the 'English' of the *Guerre de Cent Ans*.

At first glance the place seems empty, inhospitable even, with its vast horizon brooding over the huddled forests and wayward streams, framing moorland, peat bog and prairie. Yet the past whispers loudly here through its combination of worked stone, soil, trees and weather. What was the message? This is what hooked me, made me stay. The closer I looked at the landscape the more it revealed of human interaction, dating back thousands of years. Depopulated, abandoned by the tribes, it never felt lonely.

This cycle of poems was produced from a year of watching and listening to Aubrac, to nature, which in turn produced and bears witness to a part of us. It was also a year in which I underwent a cycle of chemotherapy. The prospect of death and renewal. The treatment, the seasons, the land seemed to be well acquainted. I had the privilege of observing and documenting the experience.

I

Bedrock

anti-life
we came to call Hell

raging Earth turned itself
inside out

projectile magma cooled
to a desert of lava

calmed by a worldwide sea
where continents wrench

and collide
keeled in a deeper

boiling ocean
of unquiet matter

then ice
that wrought rock

and the gentle greening
erosion provides

ice wind sun and rain
through the medium of rock

500 million years
read in lichen

work in progress
our base masterpiece

Wind

is perfecting the plateau.
After each process
the wind, scouring, smoothing—

the glacial tramlines etched
across granite and basalt
are being worked out.

I too am being perfected—
my dust will take its place
in the solar dance. The wind's

mindless work is polishing
polishing the world away
to a perfect pebble

a blue-green gem
shining in the reflective light
of heavenly bodies

become someone's moon
someone's Goddess.

Vulcania

So the roar of volcanoes commanded
the land—stone and beam
pasture and roaming beast—

this plateau, platter, served up
for proto-Celtic man
emerging from catacombed canyons,

the limestone womb. Generations
nurtured in volcanic safety
under miles of ice

entered the light with their genius
their language and art
to hunt and herd,

their collective song of survival
rhythmic, patient
from the volcano's hardened tongue

a far cry dimly heard, resounding
in the sedimented skull
the turbulent heart.

Druidic

Above the Papist spires in the valley,
above the tree-line, the stone rigging
of walls, dolmens, menhirs, cromlechs

strategically plots the plateau
claiming the uplands,
symbols and signals

that someone survived
was connecting—
a plea to fellow survivors, markers

pinning down their rough world.
And here amid the hardware
of that stone-aged effort

a vertical 'I' making marks on paper
receiving recording transmitting
logged in to a network

of recognition and need
navigating thought-time
dreamtime, claiming a space

a connection
before our sun sets
before the heart's magma cools.

Moonstone

calling up the tides
calling up molten rock

me.

A Legionnaire Arrives In Aubrac

We are the hunted we are hunting
the past outflanking
stands before me

our histories are escape routes
through time

and here we are
let loose in open fields

Lake Of Monks

When I'm sitting on a slab of pure planet
overlooking the *Lac Des Moines*
I feel my bones absorbing
stored heat. Could I sit here forever?

The lake is a great pond dug by monks
a thousand years ago to catch water
and stock with fish. Conviction men
scolding, singing, cajoling. Above all

I hear laughter—cassocks rolled up
to the knees, hairy legs and bare feet
splashing about. They will wash
in captured rain, eat trout, drink snow-melt beer.

I can also see over the lake
off the plateau far to the south
across the fuming valleys
of people chasing down a dream.

When I think of leaving
my legs object
my marrow wants to sink
into the warm depths of crystallised stone

at home in this bleak silent place
where I too was once a stranger
where laughter echoes down the centuries
                                    and monks played.

Looking up

I saw something
in the May blue—
silver-white
moth-like fly-like
moving erratically
blindly as though
hitting panes of glass
turning corners

perhaps I was
expecting a swallow
or swift to take it
when suddenly
it disappeared

I remained looking up
retracing the pattern
it had been working
the invisible lines
imprinted on the sky
for my snapshot eye
now being developed
deep in mind

the articulations
of a tiny
silver-white spirit
miming something
I should know

Transhumance

The farmers' forearms and faces
are already bronzed, armouring-up
for summer, the long days in the fields.

The cows are turning their horned heads
facing uphill, towards summer pastures.

They need to move, driven
by the memory in their bones
to breach the fences and start walking.

Leading upwards, the ancestral paths
are carrying cattle on their dreamlines

away from the fetid winter compound,
a tired, exhausted plot, too hot
and dusty now for these anxious mothers

where buzzards kites and crows
gather, circling the newborn.

What The Thunder Said

The voice of beginning and end
revered by all nature
presides over the making of matter

anti-matter, planets, rattled
the teeth of dinosaurs. I watched

the sky massing—it seemed to be
closing down over the world—
counted the seconds between flashes.

Then, that first dry guttural—
breaking news—the opening salvo
of an offensive—the birth or death
of a solar system or god—
ancestors and avatars
drumming the story through me.

Hammering beginning to end
the thunder brooked no argument
my entrails held no answers.

The plateau quaked on its root.

Out Of The Blue

Swallows are sweeping the teeming sky
scooping up insects for the nestlings
impatient in their clay coracles
cleaved to rafters, eaves,
awaiting providers, decrypting signals.

The thin thread of life
strong as steel—
at least four in five will survive.

For now blind, flightless
they thrive on the pure bounty
from out of the Aubrac blue

the teeming sky mad with life
vibrant screechings and beseechings

the mazy weave of worlds.

A Call To Prayer

Up at dawn and the doves' cooing
and counter-cooing
is a tolling half-lament
under the swallows' scherzos.

The absent-minded chimes of lauds drift
over the lonely fields, a call to prayer
to those who, replaced by machines
long ago gave up the habit.

The waking sun's stretching rays
search around behind the cloud
plumping up, assembling
above the church's solid fact

planted by monks and masons
weighed down by the saints—
stone taking root in stone—
a sounding chamber

for the centuries' wishes and hopes
of pagans and priests
where Occitan and Latin collide.
A witch's hat to cap the Kabbalah.

Still, the ground thirsts—each year
hotter, drier. The prayers
of peasants were usually for rain
and usually addressed to the dry thunder

drowning out the wailing bells of churches.

Canicule

The land breathes hard—
a summer sweltering

a heat dome from Africa
pumped up

by depression over Portugal
scorched through Spain

to settle over southern France

the baked earth crumbles
the pasture arrested

cattle stand stunned
among erratics

giant boulders
of basalt and granite

carried and shed
by country-wide ice sheets

that shaped this place
their only trace

Night Moves

While the sea-level world simmered
and slithered between drought and flood
not knowing what to make of it all
the plateau continued its planetary
cooling, under the grill of July.

I became aware of the distant
grumbling of artillery—
a long-dead Batten on The Somme
knew something was up.

Clear-cut blue night, gothic-edged
with forest suddenly smudged. Ridges
disappeared under the field-grey
of oncoming rain. Cows called through
the darkness to their young. *Abide with me.*

Advanced probing of a weather front.
Thunder passed over trailing an hour
of heavy rain and hail
the plateau received as benediction.

In a nearby gorge a phosphorous stab
revealed the black flags of vultures
drenched, hunched on a limestone ledge
like a crooked line of openings
                    into a dark interior.

Above The Fray

The caustic ingredients
of a synthetic credo
are filling the valleys.

The plateau holds, unmoored
above the infernal fog
of this human war against itself.

There came Romans, Christians—
conquest conversion
and murder in mind.

Aubrac, formed by violence
deeply-rooted
floats out above the fray.

Cicatrix

Balance of wind and tilt of wing
keep him still in the air

massive raptor hanging
over the tiny world of field life

grubs lizards
moles and mice

sickle cell heraldic
a sign a visitation

flawless forensic eyes
scanning   narrowing in

then the soundless drop
to excise a faulting body

the cowed field
mourns a sudden absence

bird and prey conjoined
in life and death

the hawk-shaped scar in the sky
takes its place among the angels

What I heard in Prades d'Aubrac—

high fluting fluttering fluctuating notes
of a small bird's song

the ash tree's leaves dry shuffling

mute fussing of a butterfly's
here-and-there soundless scrutinies
stirring the air

iron on iron of the Middle Ages
still clanging out the hours
enveloped and posted by stone

the laboured drone of a loaded bee

the ocean in all the trees

the short-circuit flit
the on-off switch of an over-heated fly
its near   far   tinnitus tic

the lone lowing of a bull
drifting down from the prairie answered by

a lazy dog-yelp
from a hamlet's hazy noonday lull

then nothing   full stop
the morning come to the end of its sentence

maybe a creak
maybe the earth creaking

and now Ingrid speaking Dutch down the line
to her mother in another world of sounds

Finally

it came all at once
a combined force
as though the front
after weeks
months of stasis
decided to move
no giveaway clues
no foretelling
no reading the runes
of build-up
no countdown
from gun-flash
to detonation
but a sudden drop
of barometric pressure

overhead
a rolling shroud
of black steel howled
rent itself to pieces
synchronised night-day
fire-phosphorescence
and massed rods of rain
marching over
the parched land regained
a coordinated campaign
of cosmic power
the doomsday
vowels of birth
cancelling speech
drowning words

trembling Nature
capitulated—
a million deaths!
only she understood
this moment of renewal

A posse of vultures

heads out
thermally drawn
to the plateau's cool dome—

lightning rod to a carcass.
They circle a blue cauldron of blue
witching up something dead.

Smart weaponry of high unerring eye
once locked-on they ride in
from beyond earth's curve

cruising black crosses
guided by hunger
and programmed precision

to strip the clinging tissue
from dead, disinterested bones.
God's rough lawmen cleaning up the prairie.

Tolls For Thee

Caught between the heft of history—
summoning of church bells to vespers—
and the timer's urgent call to the kitchen
I stand on a threshold.

As I listen to one the other insists.
The timer is saying *come quickly*
before it is too late
a call to keep the future safe.

The bells appeal to my soul—
or is it my heart?—
to get back in time with the roll
of the centuries' iron and stone.

The digital blips
are calling out my vital signs,
call me to act.
The bells plod with my blood,

calibrated footsteps
wandering towards
the chamber of origins.

A falcon

launches from the cliff
of a stone tower
glides fixed-wing

beneath a powder-blue sky
to hunt the golden fire
of August pasture where

in the after-burning
turbulence of pure air
she loses me.

Bulls stand adrift,
self-absorbed hulks of darkness
while their cows and calves romp

leg-deep in the grasses' surf of seed-heads
until October calls them
down to the winter barns.

In this local universe of systems
only I am uncertain of what next year
the rest of my life will bring.

Le Vent Du Midi

from the south worries the trees'
drying leaves, bothers the grasses
nodding furious agreement
to the promise of storms.

Chimneys howl downwards,
the biggest birds bend
into the force testing its gravity.

Eventually it brings rain
bearing pink desert sand. Hailstones
big as glass eyes blindly bounce around.

Then it sighs, exhaling
the scent of sandalwood,
salt-tinged Mediterranean airs,
ghosts of antiquity, hints of Arabia

the vanguard of Africa.

La Forêt Domaniale

There's a ticking in the woodpile
I can't ignore.
The drying bark cracks and splits
but the ticking is insistent
like a scribe scratching with his quill.

A beech beetle must be chiselling away
at my chunks of stored sunshine—its stacked
masterpiece, our bullion bars of heat
to keep us through winter. We fell
and consume—the beetle takes its fee.

On my first cut in the forest
I put my ear to the trunk of a tree
the woodsman's chain was biting into.
I heard the tree moan as it shivered—
or was it singing? I stood back amazed.

Beech gave us words—*buch, boek, book*
its creamy fine impressionable grain, its
thin bark smooth as parchment. Page and binding.
This forest has stood since the defeat of ice—
the wood age still with us. Our Good Book.

Brigands' Knoll

We were named by strangers

Romans who stole our gold
sold our children down in Rome
to pay for Caesar's
death-march across the land

pilgrims building their holy highways
stone towers and reservoirs
who hired red-crossed knights of Christ
to hunt us down

armies in the name of England
who took our herds
burned our villages to the ground

then the Industrialists who came for everything

the forest gave us shelter food and fuel
the tallest tree on the highest ridge
was our watchtower
we were almost safe again

we are still here in the shadows
in the whispering of leaves
in the silence broken
by your footfall

we will never meet
the crack-shot snap of that twig
the dead weight of your history
keeps us beyond you

and still you call us brigands

Le Vent Du Midi II

The dried-up snakeless rattles
of garlic and shallots,
strung up dead-weights,
whisper in a stiff sway.

The wind dries my pores,
my eyes. I ready to be blown
into autumn as another summer
slips out of memory

poorly reckoned as it flashed past,
a wildfire too fast
for me to latch onto.
The atoms I used to play among

slip through the mind's fingers
now too fissile, mercurial, falling
like sand in an hourglass I can't reach.
But I can greet the wind, receive its gifts.

II

A Bright Spirit Descends

At sunset the valley's darknesses
crystallise to one carbon lump
under a diamond sky.

But there, a light—a torch, a hunter—
moving downward, silently,
rays needling through the trees

seeking out the startled sparkle
of retinas, reflectors of allotted death.
Terribly, they will never make sense of this.

Further down, towards the west
nests of villages gleam like embers
trembling through the purple light

long ago forsaken
by sabre-tooth, bear,
Rome

though rumours remain of the prowling wolf.

The Auld Country

Nico's a Breton
and we're drinking local whisky
not Irish, nor Scotch—but it could be.
Cervoise was the Gaulish drink.

Romans swapped wine for beer
mutton for beef
straight lines for swirls.

Together we swirl our pools of wild alcohol
inhale the peat coming off spring water
mingled with wood smoke and flicker
from logs beginning to flame in the hearth

taste the hinterland.

Operation Mushroom

I was not despondent but in some danger
when four old friends, four Falstaffs
Guy, Dave, Mick and Jim—my own
Dad's Army—came bearing gifts from Albion—
corned beef, baked beans, Eccles cakes, Spam.
Equipped with just the mongrel tongue
they voyaged eighteen hours cramped in a car,
under The Channel and three-quarters
down Gaul, out through fog and rain
into the blue. Thus they entered Aubrac.

From above the plague village of Born
our creased-up eyes peered through the glaze
towards Spain. The Pyrenees. And there,
to the south, just beyond that ridge
The Sea of Antiquity. Higher up
through forest we found a town of forges,
the knife-making centre of the world.
Then to a gathering of the finest bulls
and cattle in all of France, cornered
by beer tents like a medieval encampment.

We drank good wine, ate *truffade*, venison and boar
and laughed and laughed for three whole days
as if we were spectators at our own
tournament, which in fact we had been
for forty years. Beguiled by Aubrac
they repacked the carriage and returned
to the gloom of the north, four cheery spirits
from a once-upon-a-time happy breed,
a goodwill mission accomplished
and never so well received.

Séance

The hunt is halted,
chainsaws fall silent
for a month of deference to the deer.

At dusk people stand by their cars
at the limits of the forest—
listening posts, edgy receptors.

The Chief is not himself,
is beside himself
the violent spirit of stag

ready to rut to mate—a male madness
a compulsion
in this moment raised to ritual.

He stokes up sound to a call
drawn from unearthly depths
that travels along the echoing temple of the valley

a throttled gargling a cut throat
breathy whistle and gasp
sacrificial a convocation

taken up by the shaggy brotherhood—
they are all in it
unseen in their domains—

arguments from an underworld
upwelling of gutturals
incomprehensible animal intelligence

coming out of the dark
defining instructing warning.
The people disperse—they have heard enough.

All Souls

Stripping winds buffet the branches.
The balding forest gives up its cover—
prescribed for survival, a killing-off.

That parade of gold and red was not
triumphant pageantry but the last dregs
of dried-up surrender
delivered on a bed of dead leaves.

The soul of the forest flees
to its winter dreams, supplanted
by a dying back, immunity
suspended, vital lymph cut off. A lack
sets in the trees. They absorb and draw

nothing, shelter nothing. Brittle black
fingers appeal dumbly to a sky
that sees everything, rains havoc
everywhere now the vanity's gone.

Animals withdraw, forsaken—
economy of movement, nourishment,
the dread imminence of winter.
They know this is a power play.

Dark days ahead. The wind drops.
A condescension.
Silence. A scarlet leaf
spirals slowly to the ground
where the abandoned spirits lie down.

GR 65

This path of faith
leads to Spain—
Compostella
the rumour of relics
Joseph of Arimathea.

But here the compass
has shaken off the north—
too much local magnetism—
other powers at play
set the dial spinning.

Is this really my route
to salvation? Wet, cold,
hungry, marching
through deceitful cloud—
to Spain?

Bells boom out
guiding me into sanctuary.
But, untethered, the waves
of sound eddy around
dangerously free.

Night draws the fog in tighter.
I shall keep going forward
vaguely downward, west,
the spectre of outlaws,
brigands, my only company.

Obelisk

At the plateau's edge, a stray arm of lava
came to the end of its reach.
Scarves of shifting mist catch in the craw
of concealed crags and gorges
where settlements cling to the smoking slopes

of stone, hewed from the well-spring of stone—
tectonic remains and reminders
of when we worked and lived by stone.
This one I thought a leaning menhir
is not leaning. Sculpted out on one side

thrusting through heather and moor,
a rock spur thumbing towards the north.
Toughened accuser, like a tortured man's tongue
beyond screaming, rooted, almost wrenching
from root with all the strangled might

of a tongue's last effort. Gesture,
a death rattle's progenitor.
Still, the cloud pours from the north
condensing its tears on the stone's shaft.
The day darkens. The valleys close.

Spirit Of Merlin

Under cover of a blue-black blanket
pierced by needle points of starlight,
witches and warlocks summon
the breath of The White Dragon.

The sun rises to shine its dazzle
on a tide of thick white mist flooding
the valleys, drowning office blocks
motels and motorways, snagging

on lava cones
weighted down with churches,
towers and monasteries
situated against the pagan.

To the south-west, unmoored
from the heedless hidden city below
a cathedral is carried away
on a swan's back into the beckoning blue.

Battle Of The Trees

Cruel the ash tree
turns not aside a footbreadth
straight at the heart runs he ...
                            Câd Goddeu

Pollarded ash looks brutal, like thick,
truncated men, henchmen, arms raised, bent
at the elbow cheering or surrendering,
colonnaded men, marches of tree men
bristling with the antennae of summer's
stripped-back shoots, lines of sentries
marking long-forgotten borders
posted down the lower slopes.

But above a thousand metres you enter
the kingdom of the beech. Ash pollen
has been found in a layer of peat
laid down between ice ages. And,
for a time the climate was tropical—
when she was young Aubrac had a seashore.

Today she has swaying forests of beech
kept at bay by the herds' grazing, defining
their prairie land. A truce with the trees.
The cattle departed in October,
the forest's bonnet by November.
Now this warning blast from the north
turns the turf to tundra. From here on
ice crystals will play on the parched air.

Polar Aubrac

Besieged by a moat of mildness—
you could almost say decadence—
the plateau is an island of white.

Moorland hardens, grasses cannot shake off
the spears of frost. Trees appear terrified.
Snow stiffens under a cold sun.

Amid the icy wind-drifted waves
up-thrusting outcrop rock, buffed black
and glossy by the glaze of winter,

speckles the snowbound prairie
like granite whales
from a great depth coming up to breathe.

The Roman Way

Armoured with layers against the cold
we walk *La Voie Romaine*, crunching over
wind-wrought snow laid out like miniature landscape—

valley gorges, mountain ranges, a desert
of sharp-ridged dunes—
for us god-giants striding a globe.

You ask me to keep watch while you pee
though there's no need—no people, only
animal tracks that could have been printed weeks ago

crossing our path onto fields spreading away
on either side like frozen wings
and the big red sun angling down

biting into drifts, bleeding shadows long
across these white folds like grieving cuts,
setting bloodily over violet, snow-free hills to the west.

Silent Fugue

Midwinter stellar solstice
is a white truce, stopped life
the palaeolithic howling
of ice ages suspended
under high pressure blue.

Summer
the valleys' hush is a mourning cortège—
deep, humane, reflective—
when all the lost children pass through.
Ceremonial midday. Too hot to murmur.

Autumn silence folds out with the night
like the first dream, like dark before
there was light. Lonely owl-hoots
travel so far without landing
they return to the owls.

Once a world war paused the steel and cordite
to hear the wisdom of its silent guns,
the emptied villages.

In the moon-blue cold of an ice-desert
there's calm in the quiet, where you can hear
earth exhaling frosted breath, resting rock
humming, the sigh of dreaming trees—
swirling music of a world adjusting. Ageing.

Blank sheets wait to catch the notes—*Stille Nacht*—
catch the sobs released by melting glaciers.

Under the gnat-like dance of the stars
the plateau is in the eye of a symphony
reflecting, staring up at its youth

                              at its present

                                        at its death.

Ski Station Brameloup

Before skiers arrive a walkie-talkie
crackles to excited life *there are deer here
and boar, I think one's been injured.
There's blood on the snow*. That winter
the station recorded minus twenty-eight.

Today it's minus ten and the north wind—
the one thing they built their settlements
against—is driving the temperature down
to Arctic glee.

While Nico grooms the pistes
I chip ice from the gantries
glittering with early morning frost,
adorning the slopes like gothic spirelets.

The sun creeps over the tips of trees
to illumine a world of crystal, inscribed
white coral. Above us the scrubbed sky
is being painted lapis lazuli.

High in the frosted forest
of the *Mons d'Aubrac*
a cathedral is being perfected.

Here snowdrifts

don't melt
they draw back into themselves
degrade passively under the attrition
of dry February sun—our winter drought.

Freezing night colludes, stiffens resolve.

But March stands in the way—
winds will shift
swing round to the south and west.

The cosmos decides—
the drifts will be abandoned, left to rot
by roadsides, under hedgerows, in ditches

fading phantoms from Earth's recurring dream—
the return of perfect winter.

Coming Through

Pockets of snow hug the contours
of the moorland flanks—hollows,
drovers' routes, the lee of drystone walls,

pilgrim paths picked out in stubborn white—
winter's last redoubts exposed, luminous
against the clumped power of emerging moor.

From a distance they are strewn casualties,
discarded hardware littering
the vast battlefield of the season's cold war

oddly out of place where the sun and moon
are teasing up the new growth
coming through, rousing insects, birds.

Difficult now to recall
the deadly grip of temperature,
the body's deep fear of extinction

a slowed heart
the fleeting stillness of midwinter,
both sides, in the balance, holding their breath.

The Promise

The record relates
in the natural detritus
below turf, lakes
peat bogs that it was
the migrating herds
shaped the uplands

checked the forest
tended the flora chose
their favoured mix
of grasses plants and herbs
to flavour the milk
of this region's kindness.

Today we hardly notice
ourselves in the epic
of transhumance, dogged
plodding life urging onward,
a flow of dreamers
in the wake of ancestors

trooping up up
to renewed pasture
where once trod neoliths
mammoths aurochs
and still roam boar and deer.

After arctic ice
snow and polar winds
the miracle of winter
the promise of summer.

Celtic Cross

Here I stand before it
upright
mother's Celtic blood
coursing through my veins

granite
stalwart
two metres tall
an ogham mark
on the grassy hillside
above the treeline
guarding its meaning
like a Gormley ghost
over London
dark angels
darkly punctuating
darkly humanising
the seemingly soulless

Leaf Mould

The wild frothings of cherry, apple,
elderberry were telling me something—
there will be new buds in the forest.
Already nostalgic for long nights and firelight
I climbed up to where winter lingered.

The ground was layered with last year's leaves—
flakes of parchment, each with a spine
and lines of private information
fingerprinted beech beech beech beech.
Crunching over the fallen dossier,

the dried-out husk of winter's chrysalis,
I came to where a spring spilt garrulously
into a stopped world, filled my bottle and sat
down on a soft cushion of fallen forest,
small and awed in that massive church of light.

Something stirred. Beneath the brittle surface
leaves were generating heat, fermenting
rebellion. The sun, having chosen sides
paid keen attention, shone approval.
Spirits were waking, rising. Ascension.

The treetops' fine frazzled nerve-end fibres
against a white sky
fingertip-tingling as the feeling returned.
The forest had come through,
could barely contain its optimism

rooted in the masticated certainty
of leaf mould and the nearing sun.
A contagion of momentum.
The fruit trees were right.

Coming Home

Divining sources
of live magma

my fevered foot soles
treading electricity
a burning levitation

take me meandering
where I would not wander

through bog and marsh
yet firmly footed

as if guided
towards an end a poem

become a Jesus
walking a sea of stone

thoughtlessly
aimlessly home

Nomadic

We forsook Ruthenia for the west
for Aubrac where we hacked out a living
with our herds and hardiness
a culture left to weather
driven north by Roman pogroms
became dukes of Brittany
followed the Conqueror to Cornwall
melted into Wales Ireland Scotland
wherever you see red hair you see us
eastern Celts following the gneiss
wired to the nuclear core magnetic
drawn through stone through strata
where ossify our offended dead where
new thunder rolls over burial grounds
over Aubrac
steel-winged vessels from the new world
glutted with weaponry
coming in over the western ocean
vapour trails paralleling cattle trails
migrant routes
                  heading for Ruthenia

Fields Of Gold

First the snow crocus—orange-yellow bowls of brightness
against the frozen negative
of winter's colour-leech

then daffodils primulas dandelions buttercups
carrying the sun's pennant
jostling above the green.

Daisies hark back to snowflakes but spring
is yellow, face upturned
in adoration of light
of heat.

Life On Earth

A wise person wrote—
we are parasites
living on the cell wall
of a larger being—
or to that effect.

Increasing tremors
are reported from
Iceland, Hawaii,
Java. Flaring nights,
this unquiet earth.

And aftermath—
the plateau, its springs
forests and gorges,
animals, people—
their fears, their dreams.

Hear my heart
pounding in its cavern.
I'm a world living
off the history
of a living world.

End Times

... all that is solid melts into air
                                    Karl Marx

In the play of Sun Moon Earth
our planet is as it was and is changing

wearing away with the light
with the seasons with time

the friction of space
and travelling through space.

Cows in their cosmic cradle
know when it's time to move.

I wake at 3 a.m. to take my medicine
and hear your rhythmic breathing

as you sleep
as you dream.

In spring there is the pledge of summer,
buds appear on the branches

my skin re-hydrates
my hair growing back.

Writing In The Dark

In a dream
we meet at night on the plateau

you sit before your masterpieces—
your animals always with you—

in my skull cave
looking out through my eyes

at the world we have
the world we have to trust

my rumbling stomach wakes me
as if about to erupt

unstable entity
a rogue bacteria

our meeting
500 million years in the making

at the mercy of an asteroid

Epigram

I.M.
Francis Nouyrigat
1929-2023, Botanist

Our Project

Tiny, fragile, bent to the small world of plants
your eyes no longer recognised humans
those looming giants. Your roots were wandering,
sometime-gypsy traders from Spain—the 'new Rigats'.

Renowned abroad you grew a garden of wildflowers
in Aubrac to reveal to your children
and their children nature's parallel cosmos
of poison and cure, myth and lore.

Edged aside by institutional minds
some called you 'difficile' and 'compliqué'.
You weren't. You were straight,
sincere, your vision perfectly clear.

Viewing us from the other end
of the microscope's lens, you would say
"the garden is the heart of our project".
Your mantra. Our only way.

Notes on the Poems

Canicule
means heatwave.

Prades d'Aubrac
is a village and Commune at the southern edge of the Aubrac plateau overlooking the Valley of the Lot. 'Prades' comes from the Occitan word 'prados', meaning prairie.

Le Vent Du Midi
is a southerly wind drawn up from the Mediterranean by the cooler air of the plateau. *The Midi* is understood to be the southern third of France.

La Forêt Domaniale
Ancient forests owned mainly by royalty and the clergy were taken over by the state after the Revolution. In Aubrac local residents still have a right to a yearly amount of wood for personal use.

Operation Mushroom
In June 2022 I was diagnosed with Non-Hodgkin's Lymphoma—cancer—and started a course of aggressive chemotherapy. Having heard on the grapevine, four of my old college friends plotted with my partner to book themselves into the village hotel in order to see me. To keep the details from me they dubbed it 'Operation Mushroom' and saw themselves as infiltrating foreign territory to give succour to one of their beleaguered own. One evening in late October there was a knock on the door and there they were.

GR65
The Grande Route 65, which passes through Aubrac, is one of the pilgrim routes of the Way of Saint James (*Jacques de Compostelle*) which leads to the cathedral of Santiago de Compostella in Galicia, northwestern Spain.

Ski Station Brameloup
Brameloup means 'call of the wolf'.

Celtic Cross
'Gormley ghost'. I had in mind Antony Gormley's London rooftop sculptures of human figures looking down on the city.

Nomadic
The Rutheni were a Celtic tribe from Ruthenia, a part of modern day Ukraine, who settled in the Aveyron. By all accounts they were tall and red-headed people, driven north by Caesar during his 'pacification' of Gaul. The people of the capital city, Rodez, are still colloquially called the 'Ruthenois'.

Writing In The Dark
Unable to sleep, this was written in the early hours of 29.4.23. Later that morning I received the news that my friend and colleague Nico had been killed in a motorbike accident during the night.

Our Project
Francis Nouyrigat, founder-creator of the *Jardin Botanique de l'Aubrac*.

Milton Keynes UK
Ingram Content Group UK Ltd.
UKHW030920190924
448484UK00004B/33

9 781788 641647